Teach Your Child To Swim: Focus On Freestyle

Written by AlyT

Teach Your Child To Swim: Focus On Freestyle

Part of the Teach Your Child To Swim series
with AlyT

DEDICATED TO

my mother **RHONDA** aka **MRS PAUL**
who taught me everything I needed to know
about life †
AND my mentor **MR TIBBS** aka **TIBBSIE** ; both
of whom helped mould me into the swimmer and
swimming teacher I am today.

Written by AlyT

© Copyright 2024 by Allison Tyson. All rights reserved.

First printing: May, 2024

Disclaimer
While we draw on our professional expertise and background in teaching learn to swim and swimming training, by purchasing and reading our products you acknowledge that we have produced this book for informational and educational purposes only. You alone are solely responsible and take full responsibility for your own wellbeing as well as the health, lives and well-being of your family and children in your care in and around water.

Stay in touch:
Born to Swim, P.O Box 6699, Cairns City, QLD 4870
SwimMechanics@yahoo.com
www.BornToSwim.com.au
www.PoweredByChlorine.com
Instagram @LearnToSwimTheAustralianWay
Etsy Store www.borntoswimglobal.etsy.com
Most titles available from Etsy, Amazon and all good online Book Retailers

Other titles by this Author:
Water Awareness Newborns
Water Awareness Babies
Water Awareness Toddlers
Learn to Swim the Australian Way Level 1 The Foundations
Learn to Swim the Australian Way Level 2 The Basics
Learn to Swim the Australian Way Level 3 Intermediate
Learn to Swim the Australian Way Level 4 Advanced
The Ultimate Pool Party Planner
Focus On Freestyle: Teaching Guide
Water Safety: Teaching Guide
Breaststroke Bootcamp: Teaching Guide
Butterfly Bootcamp: Teaching Guide
Backstroke Bootcamp: Teaching Guide
Learning To Float: Color Me In & Learn To Swim Activity Book
A Float For Every Stroke: Teaching Body Position
Visual Aids For Inclusive Aquatic Education: 100+ Swimming Flashcards
Welcome To Swim Squad: Activity Book For Swimmers
Water Safety Workbook: Activity Book For Swim Kids
Eat Pray Swim: A Swimmer's Logbook & Prayer Journal
Thalassophile: Logbook & Journal For Lovers Of The Ocean and Sea
Competitive Swimming Quotes: Coloring Book For Adults & Teens
Wild Swimming Quotes: Coloring Book For Adults & Teens
Mermaids: Coloring Book For Adults & Teens
Powered By Chlorine : Logbooks & Journals For Swimmers

A QUICK G'DAY TO ALL MY FELLOW FREESTYLERS,

Welcome to Born To Swim's FOCUS ON FREESTYLE

We've gathered together the best of teaching FREESTYLE from our LEARN TO SWIM THE AUSTRALIAN WAY series
+ some BONUS MATERIAL to help you hone into FREESTYLE BUILDING !!

Whether you're a SWIMMING TEACHER or SWIM PARENT we've made it supa easy to navigate the waters of teaching freestyle...
to just about anyone!

We've created this teaching guide to help teachers of swimming teach GENERIC FREESTYLE - freestyle that has a fast six-beat kick and long, slow arm turnover. Over time, and with training and proper coaching, swimmers should adapt their stroke to suit what is most comfortable to them.

As I always say, swimming the length of the pool isn't the ultimate marker of success. Sure, it's impressive, but if your swimmer is FLOUNDERING by the time they touch the wall, taper the distance back a bit!!
What really counts is PROPER FORM GOOD TECHNIQUE, it's all about quality over quantity when it comes to swimming.

Try the drills & BUILD THE SKILL before hammering out a mountain of laps.

And don't forget the golden rule: praise and encouragement go a long way. Celebrate every stroke, every kick, and every improvement; but don't be shy to correct mistakes and revisit learning to get that
technique perfect!

Let's dive in,

Aly T

PS. To get the most out of this book, swimmers need to feel comfortable floating and diving down under the water.

SAFETY FIRST!

⚠️ Never swim alone

⚠️ Always keep children within arms reach

⚠️ Remove distractions when teaching in water

⚠️ Never force a swimmer under the water

⚠️ Do not play breath holding games or encourage holding the breath for long periods of time

✓ Learning to swim in shallow, waist depth water is best for beginners

✓ Learning CPR & First Aid Saves Lives

POSITION 11 FLOAT

Why do it?

Body positioning is crucial to swimming freestyle correctly and minimising excess drag or resistance from the water. The Position 11 Float puts the swimmer in the ideal starter body position for building the stroke: long, straight and flat.

How to do it?

1. Stretch out flat on the water and extend your arms forward with legs behind you, keeping your feet together and toes pointed
2. Squeeze your elbows against the side of your head and look straight down
3. Hands should be shoulder distance apart and in line with the shoulders, just below the surface
4. Flex the wrists so your fingertips are pointing slightly downward

TIP

Don't hold your breath when your face is in the water. Release a steady stream of bubbles out your nose and mouth to help you relax.

stay taut, NOT tense

CHALLENGE

Practise pushing off from the wall to float. Use the momentum of your glide to help lift your legs to the surface with your hamstrings and stomach muscles. The challenge is to stay flat and on the surface with minimal resistance from the water

KICKBOARD HOLD

How to do it?

Make a little crocodile with your hand and firmly clasp the kickboard by placing your fingers on top and thumbs underneath.

TIP
Keep your eyes looking straight down and arms fully extended to avoid problems later

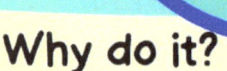

Why do it?
The 'Crocodile Hold' puts the hands & arms in the correct arm entry position, assists with shoulder flexibility and encourages swimmers to 'keep their elbows up'

Did you know?
Kickboards aren't a buoyancy device; they're tools to help swimmers balance & position themselves correctly in the water.
They're also great for learning stroke timing, aligning the shoulders, arms & hands, using the correct amount of hand & arm tension and encouraging correct arm extension. BUT only if held correctly!!
Watch out for bent arms when holding a kickboard, it can cause problems later on, like crossing the midline, dropping the elbows, lack of arm extension, or not catching the water effectively.
Another thing to avoid is looking forward at the kickboard while swimming or kicking. This can lead to lifting the head to breathe. Lifting the head can cause the swimmer's body to see-saw in the water; they'll get more tired lifting their head to breathe as their legs start to sink and body positioning collapses.

FLUTTER KICK

ledge kicking

Why do it?

The Flutter Kick helps keep the swimmer streamlined and is the most efficient & propulsive way of kicking when swimming freestyle. BUT only if performed correctly!

How to do it?

1. Lay down flat in shallow water and hold onto the submerged step or the bottom of the pool.
2. Extend and float your legs to the surface as you point your feet behind you.
3. Point your toes and use your hamstrings to lift and lower each leg, kicking from the hip', one leg at a time.
(like a pair of scissors without over-bending the knees)
4. Practise looking straight down and blowing out a stream of bubbles as you kick
5. Stop kicking and float your legs when you need to take a breath or have a rest

TIP

Keep your legs long, ankles relaxed & feet 'floppy'. Imagine you're 'kicking your socks off' as you kick

TRY THIS

Lots of practice is the secret to a strong kick. Extend your arms and hold onto the wall to 'Wall Kick'. Focus on keeping your body flat and stable as you work on a powerful, 'hip-driven' kick

wall kicks

practise your upkick too!!

KICKBOARD KICKING

How to do it?

Use the Crocodile Hold to lay flat on the surface and kick with a kickboard
Your arms must stay locked, straight and shoulder distance apart with eyes looking straight down. To ensure you are is using the correct hand & arm tension, the kickboard should stay flat on the surface with a firm grasp as you kick.

TIP

If the swimmer has no traction or propulsive power, revisit teaching the Flutter Kick. Look for over-bent knees, stiff legs & ankles and toes NOT pointed

keep the hips, heels & head at the surface

unaided kicking

Why do it?

Kicking with a kickboard helps swimmers learn to maintain the correct horizontal body positioning as they balance and move through the water with 'arms out front'.
Extending forward, with straight arms will strengthen both the core and the kicking technique.
Swimmers should also practise kicking without a board to ensure they can maintain a flat, horizontal bodyline on the surface of the water, without an aid, and stay relaxed as they kick

POSITION 11 KICKING

keep the hips, heels, head & hands at the surface

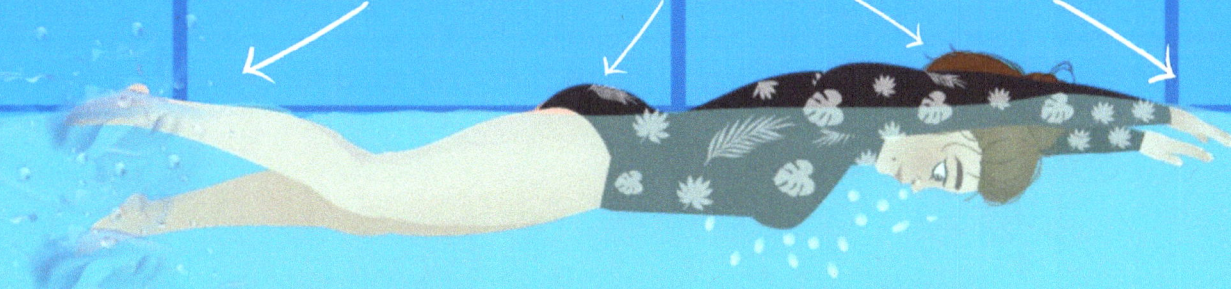

How to do it?

1. Stretch out flat on the water and Position 11 Float
2. Keep your elbows squeezed against the side of your head and look straight down
3. Your hands should be apart and in line with your shoulders, just below the surface of the water
4. Flex your wrists and point the fingertips slightly downward as you reach forward and kick

Why do it?

Before adding the arms and breathing, Position 11 Kicking helps imprint muscle memory of the ideal body positioning for swimming freestyle. Without the aid of the kickboard, the swimmer will need to use their core and arm tension to maintain the positioning of their arms stretched out front as they kick.

TIP Kick short distances to discourage the need to lift the head to take a breath

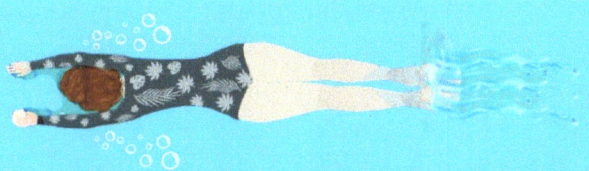
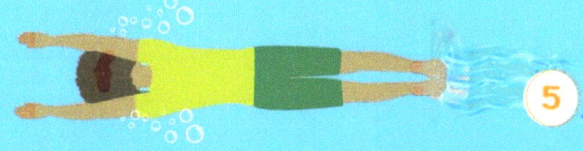

SUPERMAN KICKING

How to do it?
1. Stretch out flat on the water and extend one arm forward in line with your shoulder, pressed against the side of your head. This is your 'LEAD ARM'
2. The wrist of your LEAD ARM should be slightly flexed with fingertips angled slightly downward
3. Rest your other arm against the side of your body with the thumb pressed against your thigh
4. Look straight down & keep your body flat at the surface of the water
5. Your Legs should be straight out behind you as they perform a strong Flutter Kick

lead arm

lead arm

Why do it?
Superman Kicking helps imprint muscle memory of the ideal hand entry and exit positions for swimming freestyle. The swimmer will need to use their core and arm tension to maintain the positioning of the arms as they kick.

TIP
Keep the feet close together & big toes brushing past each other to keep the kick tight and core muscles engaged

FEEL FOR THE WATER

How to do it?

Stand or sit in the water and very slowly move your hands through the water like you are doing Tai Chi or conducting an orchestra.

Keep your hands firm, not tense, and feel for the weight of the water as your hands continuously move and change direction

Move your hands in a sideways 'figure 8' direction ∞ and feel for the pressure of the water against your hands

Extend your arm and enter the hand fingertips first, then bend your elbow and push the water behind you

Lastly, try laying on the side of the pool, extend one arm into the water, entering the hand fingertips first and bending the elbow to push the water behind you

Why do it?

Learning to move the water effectively with your hands and forearms is often overlooked when learning to swim. When a swimmer knows what to feel for as they swim, they will have a more effective 'catch' and apply pressure at the right moments during the stroke; instead of slipping and slicing through the water with no traction.

bend before you press

TIP

The more time spent in the water sculling, playing or doing water aerobics, the better your feel for the water will become

FREESTYLE ARMS

Why do it?
Dryland practise with a kickboard will help the swimmer learn the correct direction and cues for turning the arms over during the pull and recovery phases of freestyle.

Choose your recovery
There are numerous ways to recover the arms over the water during freestyle. Swimmers will most often lean towards the method that feels most comfortable to them. It is important to note that the bent elbow or high elbow recoveries, if not performed properly, can lead to shoulder injuries and 'hand-led' freestyle. Therefore, it is advisable to teach a straighter arm recovery, known as "Rainbow Arms" or 'Gull Wings'.

TIP
Swivelling the torso at the hips and 'opening up' the armpits will help greatly to get the arms to recover easier behind you

How to do it?
1. Stand in the water, look straight ahead and Crocodile Hold a kickboard above your head
2. Keep both arms straight with your elbows touching the side of your head
3. Release one hand, keeping the arm straight as it passes downward in front of you to the side of your leg
4. The thumb of the moving arm should brush the side of your thigh before the arm swings around, behind you, to re-hold the kickboard
5. Repeat the arm circle movement with the other arm

POWER TRIANGLES

Challenge
Float or kick with a kickboard in 'Position 11' and alternate one arm at a time moving your arms slowly into the 'Power Triangle' position

Why do it?
Power Triangles are the secret weapon to a powerful underwater 'pull phase' of swimming each of the competitive strokes. A 'Power Triangle' reduces the likelihood of swimmers slicing, wiping or slipping through the water with no traction.

TIP
The elbow must ALWAYS stay higher than the hand as the arm moves under the water from directly out front to our side

practise with a kickboard

POSITION 11 FREESTYLE

Why do it?
Position 11 Freestyle helps develop a coordinated, balanced and horizontal stroke by keeping the arms extended out front, and focus on pulling themselves forward with each stroke whilst maintaining a strong kick. Swimmers also learn to engage the right muscles, move various body parts and maintain proper form by keeping their arms shoulder-width apart, extending forward, and pulling in a straight line back to the hips as they kick.

practise with a kickboard

TIP
Use the rotation of your shoulders to swing your arms over the water

How to do it?

1. Start in Position 11 Float and start kicking
2. Reach forward with both arms and pull the water behind you by bending one arm and pushing the water all the way back to your hip
3. As the hand approaches the hip, move the hip out of the way by rotating the hip upward, out of the water
4. As the hip rotates upwards, the lead arm should extend further forward and the travelling arm should exit the water ELBOW first and swing (recover) over the water
5. As the recovering arm arches over the water the hand should redirect forward, after passing over the shoulder, and enter fingertips first; followed by the wrist, then the elbow before extending and returning to the Position 11 starting position

SIX KICKS SWITCH

Why do it?

Six Kicks Switch teaches the swimmer coordination skills as they swap lead arms, correct timing of the 'opposite arms' and hand entry & exit positioning whilst maintaining a strong kick and horizontal body position.

How to do it?

1. Start in the Superman Kicking position
2. Kick six strong kicks then switch the lead arm and kick six more kicks
3. It is important the arm at the side, the 'back arm', begins it's recovery BEFORE your lead arm starts to pull
4. Always 'keep one arm out front' and kick hard

TIP

Don't forget to exhale when the face is in the water!

open your armpits

STATIONARY SIDE BREATH

How to do it?

1. Stand or sit in shallow water holding a kickboard or the side of the pool with one hand.
2. Place your face into the water, look straight down and straighten your arm as it rests against the side of your head
3. Turn your face, leading with your chin, so you are looking across the surface of the water and your head rests against the shoulder of your extended (lead) arm
4. The shoulder of your opposite arm should rotate upward out of the water as you turn your head
5. Only the shoulders and head should move when you take each breath

TIP
Keep one eye in the water when you turn to breathe and press your ear into the water

head resting against the lead arm

Why do it?

When swimming freestyle, if something goes wrong with the stroke, it typically occurs during breathing. The key is to stay horizontal without disrupting the stroke by lifting the head. Stationary Breathing highlights and isolates turning the head to breathe

ear in the water

FREESTYLE ROTATION

Why do it?

Horizontal rotation with kicking ie the 'corpse drill' or 'head-led kicking' teaches swimmers to use their shoulders and torso to roll the body from side to side. Rolling (or rocking) from side to side makes it easier for the swimmer to get their arms out of the water during the recovery phase of freestyle, adds power to the stroke and will help maintain a horizontal body position when it comes time to take a breath to the side

draw your belly button in

Challenge

As the kick & rotation skills develop, challenge swimmers to kick on their front, without rolling onto their back for air. Instead, encourage them to stay horizontal and keep as much of their face in the water as possible. The challenge is to breathe on their side, not onto their back

TIP
If you need too, use fins to assist with this drill

How to do it?

1. Begin by kicking on your back with your arms by your sides
2. Roll onto your front using only your shoulders, core and kick
3. Continue to exhale as you use your shoulders, core & kick to roll onto your back, staying as flat as you can
4. Remember, the head moves with the body, staying in a neutral position (no lifting or tilting) with each roll

KICK ON SIDE BREATH

TIP
Do not slow or pause the kick when taking a breath

practise with a kickboard

shoulder up!

Why do it?
Lifting the head as the swimmer moves through the water disrupts the stroke and unbalances the swimmer, whereas learning to turn the head and roll onto their side keeps the swimmer in the ideal horizontal position as they swim

How to do it?
1. Push off from the wall on your side, with your face looking straight down and lead arm extended out front
2. Similar to the 'Superman Kick' position but this time with your shoulder (opposite the lead arm) out of the water
3. Once balance has been established, rotate the head to breathe a QUICK breath whilst maintaining a strong kick
4. When taking a breath, the LEAD ARM should reach further forward as you roll the opposite shoulder upwards out of the water. The back of your head should touch the side of your lead arm
5. Return the face STRAIGHT DOWN after each quick breath

Did you know?
Stable swimmers can balance on their lead arm, unstable swimmers tend to lift the head and press down on their lead arm

BUBBLE & BREATHE

TIP
Do not let the kickboard wiggle or move from straight out in front

Why do it?
Using a kickboard to isolate the breathing arm and bubble arm will aid the swimmer in synchronising the freestyle body movements with the timing of the breath and help establish the correct rhythm.

breathing arm

bubble arm

How to do it?

1. Sit or kick with a kickboard using the Crocodile Hold. Ensure your arms are straight and resting against the side of your head.
2. Let go of the kickboard with one hand. The arm continuing to hold the kickboard is your BUBBLE ARM, your other arm is your BREATHING ARM
3. As your BREATHING ARM lets go of the kickboard and begins to push the water behind you, start turning your head, rolling to the side to take a quick breath
4. As your BREATHING ARM reaches the thigh it is time to return your face back into the water
5. When your BREATHING ARM grasps the kickboard your BUBBLE ARM begins its cycle and it is time to exhale
6. Remember to keep the kick constant throughout the cycling of bubble and breathing; breathe only during the BREATHING ARM's cycle

CATCH-UP FREESTYLE

How to do it?

1. Start kicking in Position 11 with both arms extended out front
2. Begin Bubble Arm & Breathing Arm by switching arms one at a time to pull and recover over and under the water

You must maintain one arm out front at all times as each arm completes its cycle. Each arm waits for the other arm to 'catch up' BEFORE it starts its cycle

3. When the recovering Bubble Arm enters the water, fingertips first, the head should begin to turn to get a quick breath as the Breathing Arm begins its cycle.
4. Your face should return to the water BEFORE the Breathing Arm finishes its cycle

Maintain a strong kick throughout the stroke cycle.
Do not hold your breath!

BONUS TIP
A breath taken too slow or a pause in kicking leads to sinking

Why do it?
After mastering the balance and coordination of their kick with arm movements, the next step to building a more efficient freestyle is to establish a connection between body rotation, breath timing, and the phases of the arm cycle.

reach forward
pull to breathe

TIP
Keep the extended arm reaching forward and hands shoulder-width apart at all times

CAT & MOUSE FREESTYLE

TIP: Revisit each activity to reinforce & perfect your freestyle technique

Why do it?

Many swimmers 'fall over' their lead arm when taking a breath, causing them to become unbalanced, lift their head, shorten their stroke, drop their elbows etc. Cat and Mouse Freestyle aims to transition gradually from Position 11 Catch-Up Freestyle toward swimming a well-balanced, supported freestyle.

- one eye in, one eye out
- thumb to thigh
- toes pointed
- lead arm support
- ear in the water

How to do it?

In this technique, the hand of the arm used for breathing is called the Cat, while the hand of the arm as you blow bubbles is the Mouse.
The goal is to prevent the Cat hand from 'catching up' to the Mouse hand and vice versa.

1. Start by pushing off the wall and swim using Position 11 Catch-Up Freestyle
2. As you build momentum, gradually reduce the pause between each arm cycle by starting the pull of the hand out front just before the recovering arm re-enters the water.
3. Experiment with timing, ensuring you maintain support from your lead arm while breathing.

Freestyle
LESSON PLAN

Activities
Equipment: Kickboard, Fins (optional)

Activities Completed

- Position 11 Float
- Kickboard Hold
- Flutter Kick
- Kickboard Kicking
- Position 11 Kicking
- Superman Kicking
- Feel For The Water
- Freestyle Arms
- Power Triangles
- Position 11 Freestyle
- Six Kicks Switch
- Stationary Side Breath
- Freestyle Rotation
- Kick On Side with Breath
- Bubble & Breathe
- Catch-Up Freestyle
- Cat & Mouse Freestyle

Thank you for diving into the world of swimming with us!
We hope you've enjoyed splashing through the pages and discovering new aquatic skills. Your feedback is invaluable to us. If you enjoyed our books, please consider leaving a review or share your experience with others. Happy swimming and thank you for being a part of our
#SwimmingRevolution

www.ingramcontent.com/pod-product-compliance
Lightning Source LLC
Chambersburg PA
CBHW041526070526
44585CB00002B/104